MY INCREDIBLE JOURNEY

Ossie Langfelder

TABLE OF CONTENTS

DEDICATION

Written July 23, 1999

Our lives are guided by the way we endure the many trials and tribulations we encounter during our lifetime. It is not just our focus which enables us to become achievers, but rather the people who love and support us which allows us to appreciate the great benefits of life. I, therefore, dedicate this book to my Mother and Father, who guided, educated and protected me during extremely difficult times of my youth, prior to World War II.

And to my wife, Midge, and our thirteen children, all of whom shared many adversities with me, but always shared so much love which I am certain no one else ever experienced. This is really their story, since they made my incredible journey possible. My cup, truly, runneth over!

PROLOGUE

I am glad to have the opportunity to give you a little impression what it means for people to leave all behind, to lose all, and to go out in a strange world.

I was born in the city of music, Vienna, the capital of Austria, where all the great musicians, like Johann Strauss, Franz Schubert, Ludwig Van Beethoven, and many others lived. Vienna is a city where the world's famous waltz, *The Blue Danube*, by Johann Strauss was composed.

Because of my life's unique circumstances, memories of my youth are very vivid. My sister, Edith, and I had very strict parents while being raised in one of Vienna's middle class neighborhoods. We lived on the second floor of a four story apartment building. My Mother dedicated her life to both of us, from educational studies, entertainment and taking us to the park several times a week.

I was six years of age when I started public school and attended for four years. After public school, each pupil who would like to attend a special high school, had to undergo an examination. One had to attend eight grades and take twelve subjects, among them French, Latin, or English. We were compelled to take all these subjects. It was not possible to learn music or to play any games at school. We had to be respectful to the teachers and had to stand when the teacher addressed us or when we spoke to the teacher. Boys and girls went to separate schools. The school started at eight o'clock in the morning and was completed at five o'clock. We had a lot of homework to do and did not have any study periods. On Saturdays, school was dismissed at twelve o'clock.

It was generally forbidden for children under the age of sixteen to attend movies, except on Saturday when there were special performances for the children in a few theaters.

Vienna, with its beautiful surroundings of high hills and mountains, allowed us in wintertime to go skiing, sledding, and skating. Vienna was a lovely and modern city, with two million people, which enjoyed a happy existence until March 11, 1938, when the Germans marched in and invaded Austria, stealing and robbing all they could. The change came so suddenly, we could not realize what was happening to us. It was like we had learned as the Huns came from Asia to Europe centuries ago. They took all away they could, burned churches and temples, killed clergy and rabbis because they believed in God and did not agree with the Nazis. Thousands of people from Vienna were sent to con-centration camps where many of them perished. I remember the case of Pastor Niemoellor, who, even though he was a Lutheran minister, was sent to a concentration camp.

In 1939, we left Austria for Zurich, the capital of Switzerland, after I attended three grades in high school. Switzerland is a very beautiful country, with high mountains and many lakes. The schools are similar to those in Austria. My sister and I stayed in Switzerland for two months, for the first time in our lives separated from our parents, who flew to London to get the permit for us to come to England because we both did not have a permit. You can believe me, it was very, very hard to live with strange people and to know that your parents are so far away. I was always glad when we got a letter, and the first two weeks we both had swollen eyes because we were crying the whole night long. It was our happiest day when we got a wire that the permit was finally granted and we could come to England.

On May 24, 1939, we flew to the capital of England, London. I won't forget as we left the plane, we recognized our parents on the roof of the restaurant at the airfield in Croydon. London is a very interesting and old city. It has many historical buildings, some of which I saw. The *Tower of London* was used as a prison in previous times, and now as a prison for traitors and spies. Nearby was the famous *Tower Bridge*. I visited *Westminster Abbey*, saw the Parliament with it's *Big Ben* and heard its famous "*Play of Bells*". After two weeks, I was sent to the *St. Aloysius College* where

I had to learn the English language, because I could not speak even a word of English. I had a hard time because we could not understand each other. After one month, though, I could understand a little, but not speak much. Nobody could speak my own language, so I had to learn English very quickly. I had really nice schoolmates who were very helpful and polite to me in our free time. They always taught me a few words. The Brothers always tried to make me happy because I felt very sad at first. I learned to play tennis and the national game of England, Cricket.

The life was very simple in the school. We had to get up at 7:15 A.M., get dressed quickly, and go to our breakfast table. Five minutes after breakfast, we started to school. The lessons in England were very easy and the teachers were not very strict.

After attending the school in London for three months, the war started and we were evacuated to a small town nearly 200 miles away from London, called Wisbech. Each boy came to a family and lived there with them for one year. I had a lot of fun and a very nice time. I joined the Boy Scouts, played Cricket often, and went for many bicycle rides. Once I saw the wreckage of a German plane, which was shot down by one of the famous British *Spitfires*. All the pilots were killed.

Every two or three months my parents came to see me. One day I got a wire which told me to come immediately to London. I went there and was told that we were leaving London for the

United States. I cried with one eye and laughed with the other, because on the one hand, I wanted to stay, and on the other, I wanted to travel.

On August 16, 1940, we left England from Liverpool aboard the *Duchess of Atholl,* and after seven days, we landed in Montreal, Canada. We had 1,300 English children on board. The voyage was very pleasant and interesting. We saw whales and icebergs and our ship was accompanied by destroyers and four planes of the English Navy for three and a half days. After six days, we saw land again. It was a part of Newfoundland. The voyage on the St. Lawrence River was very enjoyable and we passed by Quebec.

On Sunday August 26, 1940, we arrived at the *Pennsylvania Station* in New York City, in "God's Country". New York is a beautiful city with its skyscrapers and straight streets. I saw the *Empire State Building*, the highest in the world, and *Rockefeller Center* with its *Radio City*. I went to *Central Park* and visited the zoo and I saw the *Statue of Liberty*. All this was very impressive.

We lived in New York for three months before going to Chicago, where we stayed only two weeks. Then, we traveled to Springfield, where we will stay forever!

After the past few years, I am really glad that we have such a nice place where the people are so friendly and pleasant. It is not only a compliment, but we all, my parents, my sister and myself, are very happy to live here. We like Springfield and its people best and we especially like our school, *Lanphier High School.* I hope to become a good citizen of America and my daily prayer ends always, "God bless America and give England the victory!"

Written by me, Ossie Langfelder, in 1941.

CHAPTER 1
REMINISCING: THE BEGINNING

June 27, 1998:

We were riding in our son-in-law's, Jim, and our daughter's, Jamie, luxurious air-conditioned van to Florida. Their youngest son, Jonathan, was sleeping in the back seat. Midge and I were relaxing in the middle of the van, occasionally looking at the state of Georgia's scenery, while we were watching the movie *Air Force One* on TV.

It is a very traumatic and intense movie about terrorists hijacking the President's plane, brutally killing several on board and harassing the President's thirteen year old daughter. While I was watching this scared and intimidated little girl, it brought back some bitter memories to mind, as I felt tears swelling in my eyes.

Although I started writing my autobiography some years ago, I felt compelled to complete it after watching this emotionally packed movie. It reminded me of a day in April, 1938, when as a boy of eleven, I walked with my Dad hand in hand for well over eighteen hours throughout Vienna, in order to avoid my Dad being arrested and sent to a concentration camp for his Jewish beliefs.

With this in mind, I decided to complete writing my life story, as I still remember it. This book is for our thirteen children and their many offspring, not as a memorial to me, but rather that all of them may understand and enjoy their lives to the fullest. I dedicate this autobiography to the four people who shaped my life with their love and understanding: Mom, Popsch, Grosse Omama, and Midge. Few people in this world have had the many good fortunes and opportunities which I have experienced.

Mom

Popsch

Grosse Omama

Midge

1926 was a year which saw the birth of Elizabeth II, Queen of England, The Reverend Ralph Abernathy, and none other than Marilyn Monroe. It was the year Rudolph Valentino, Annie Oakley, and Claude Monet died. It was a year the first woman, Gertrude Ederle, swam the English Channel, and Roger Hornsby managed the *St. Louis Cardinals*, while Greta Garbo came to *MGM Studios* from Sweden. It was a year which brought religious prejudices to the forefront, when Irving Berlin, of Jewish descent, married a Roman Catholic, Ellin Mackay and, oh yes, it was the year of my birth!

I was born August 2, 1926 to a Lutheran mother and Jewish father in a predominately Catholic country. Upon my birth, I already had a fifteen month old sister, Edith, which was to comprise our entire family. I always felt I had the good fortune of being born in Vienna, Austria, famous for its culture, music, and beauty. I was delivered in a private sanatorium in Vienna, Austria into an above average income family. My Mother would never have allowed anyone to take her to a public or general hospital. Because she encountered some difficulty in the delivery, my Mother named me Oswald after the Doctor she claimed saved our lives.

I was greeted and, I surmise, welcomed, not only by the Doctor and nurses, my Mother, Ruth Maria, and my Father, Otto, but also by my fifteen month old sister, Edith. Of course I do not recollect any part of this auspicious occasion.

Although I have forgotten the names of the few individuals I had known in my childhood, I can vividly remember some of the joys and hardships of growing up in Vienna. I was born to Ruth Maria and Otto Berthold Langfelder. Both my parents were twenty-five years old at the time, having been born in December and August respectively.

My Father and Mother and I.

My Father was manager of a paper manufacturing company, while my Mother was a private secretary in a law firm until the birth of my sister. I was nurtured by Nana Krainz, a distant aunt of my Mother's, with the help of my maternal Grandmother, Grosse Omama. Both lived in the same apartment building as us, with the exception of residing on different floors.

From this day forward, while in Vienna, we lived at thirty-three *Hutteldorfer Strasse* (street), fifteenth *Bezirg* (district). Austria was, at that time, about the size of Illinois, with a population of a little more than six million. The majority of its inhabitants were of the Catholic faith. I was born into a mixed marriage family, which did not have the blessing or approval of either my maternal Lutheran Grandmother or paternal Jewish Grandparents. Mixed marriages were frowned upon by everyone during the first part of this century.

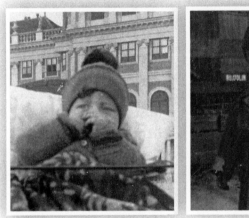

As a toddler in Vienna, Austria.

Only pictures left to me by my Mother refresh my memory of some aspects of life prior to my sixth birthday. Because of unique circumstances, memories of my youth are very vivid. My sister, Edith, and I had very strict parents, while being raised in one of Vienna's middle class neighborhoods. We lived on the second floor of a four story building.

My Mother's mother lived on the fourth floor by herself, but spent most of the time with us in our apartment, cooking, doing dishes, and other chores which my Mother apparently did not wish or choose not to do. Though I remember very little prior to the age of six, I do recall my Grandmother always bathing us in a portable tub in the middle of the kitchen and Mother drying us thoroughly. Our Grandmother was always cautious not to allow soap to run in our eyes, since I recall screaming when our Mother washed our hair.

Our Mother was a very attractive, sophisticated, and an immaculate woman who spent her early years taking care of Edith and me, while continually cleaning our two room apartment, which was furnished with nothing but white furniture. Dirt was her number one enemy and supreme cleanliness was our every day environment. Our Mother would take us to the park, feed us meals prepared by her Mother and very seldom leave Edith and I out of her sight.

My Mother and I

In the streets of Vienna in 1928.

My Father, Otto, 3rd from left, and his hockey team.

My Father climbing the Alps Mountains.

Our Father was an excellent athlete. He played ice hockey on the *Vienna Hakoah Team* from 1927 to 1933 and refereed international hockey from 1933 to 1938. My Father also enjoyed swimming, sledding and soccer. Growing up, I remember my Dad as a strict disciplinarian with me. I always felt he was much tougher on me than my sister, Edith.

The first recollection I have of my childhood, is the first day my Father and Mother took me to school. I vividly remember screaming at the top of my lungs, since I apparently was afraid to stay at school without my parents. That, I know, had to be difficult on my Mother, since she did not leave me at school, but took me back home. However, the second day was not to be as kind to me and I remained in school.

Schools, at that time, were segregated, educating boys in one room and girls in the other. We attended school five and a half days a week, having the same teacher for the first four years. School did not seem as difficult as coming home and having to do homework. Our Mother sat with us every evening to make certain we completed our studies as required. Our handwriting had to be perfect and erasure marks were not permitted. My Mother destroyed many handwritten papers she felt were less than perfect.

My school and classmates in Vienna.

I am the first boy on the left in the middle section.

My Grandmother, Kleine Omama and my Grandfather, Opapa.

My Father, who had a younger brother, Fritz, came from a very affluent family. His mother, Ida Maier, of Czechoslovakian descent, and his father, Berthold Langfelder, of Austrian and Hungarian descent, were the owners of a shirt manufacturing company. My Grandmother, only about five foot in height, managed the daily operation, while my Uncle Fritz, who was single and lived with my grandparents, was the company's pattern maker and form cutter.

Fritz could cut upwards of 150 cotton cloths with a wooden form on top by hand with an extremely sharp, long bladed knife. No mechanical devices existed for this purpose and very few people had the strength or capability to accomplish such a feat. Fritz was a man about five feet, six inches tall with muscles, which would put any weightlifter to shame. After cutting several hundred forms a day, seamstresses would then sew the shirts for the final product to be delivered to numerous men's clothing stores in Vienna. Fritz was single and worked in the factory six days a week. I remember my Grandmother was very dependent and very demanding of him, but she always seemed to be more affectionate to my Dad.

By now, I am certain one is wondering why I had not spoken of my Dad's father. Although my Grandmother and Uncle Fritz worked all day in the factory, my Grandfather, Berthold Langfelder, always elegantly dressed, came to the factory only once a day. He would go early in the morning to unlock the factory, and when my Uncle Fritz came to work, he would depart to go to the *Kafe Haus*, not to be seen the rest of the day. He was truly a very affluent, extremely well-dressed, strict, successful and demanding gentleman. While men today pass their time on the golf course, men of prestige and affluence spent their leisure time in the privacy of their *Kafe Haus* playing cards, smoking, sipping mocha, or reading.

My Opapa, Edith and I.

My Mother, born to parents with above average income, suffered great financial difficulties when her father, who traveled extensively in Russia as a salesman, was arrested by the Russians during World War I. Her mother, unemployed and forced to raise two daughters and a son during Grandfather's imprisonment, experienced many hardships. He was caught by the Russians shortly after the start of World War I, and being suspected of spying, was sent to a Siberian prison. He escaped in 1918 and was able, due to speaking fluent Russian and having a few Russian acquaintances, returned to Vienna after the war ended. He had, however, contracted respiratory problems while being in prison and died a short time after his return.

I don't believe my Mother ever overcame the shock over his imprisonment and his early death. She spoke of him frequently with great love, compassion, and pride, and a sparkle in her eyes. My Mother was an extremely proud and sophisticated lady.

August Oscar Dengler,

my Mother's Father,

who died before I was born.

Mom's mother, Maria Dengler, was also of German descent. She lived on the fourth floor in our apartment building and on a daily basis came to our two room apartment to cook and generally do housekeeping duties. We called her "*Grosse*" (large) Omama, since she was much bigger than my Father's mother, whom we called "*Kleine*" (little) Omama.

Grosse Omama and I were very close, while in no uncertain terms, my sister, Edith, was certainly Kleine Omama's favorite.

Our tidy, immaculate, two room apartment, located in a four story apartment complex, in which every apartment had to share a bathroom with their neighbor apartment, was in those days, considered quite luxurious.

The bathroom consisted only of a stool, a sink and two metal tubs, which hung on opposite walls. Every time a bath was taken, the tub was removed and brought into the kitchen, where the tub was filled with hot water, heated on the stove by my Grandmother, and then poured into the tub. Our Grandmother would then bathe us individually while my Mother would prepare to dry us, and then our Mother would dress us. As I recall, this was an enjoyable procedure, except when our Mother washed our hair and the soap ran into our eyes. My Mother was not very sympathetic, although Grosse Omama (Big Granny), was usually present with a towel. I felt my Mother appeared to be more gentle with my sister, Edith.

My maternal Grandmother lived in a one room efficiency, as I recall, on the fourth floor of the same apartment building. My Father, I understood, paid for her expenses, since she had been widowed, and since she cooked, baby-sat, and did many chores for us. Although she was very strict, I loved my Grandmother dearly, since she was always good and seemed to cater to me.

There seemed to be a personality conflict between Edith and Grosse Omama, although in those days, we just said "they did not get along". Edith was always closer to our paternal grandparents, who usually catered to her every whim.

Since Kleine Omama (Little Granny), Ida Maier, only had two sons, I surmised she enjoyed Edith visiting her, since she never had a daughter to cuddle. She was always very nice to me. Although at a very young age, I realized Edith was her favorite, since she was generally allowed to go to their luxurious apartment and even stay overnight, which never appeared to be my good fortune.

My paternal Grandparents, being very affluent, lived on a third floor of another apartment building. It was located in a four story apartment building around the corner from us on *Bein Gasse* (Bone Street). I don't remember how many rooms were in the apartment, but I can vividly recall a grand piano in a very spacious living room, a dining room, and their very own bathroom with a bathtub. It was a very special treat for me when I was permitted to visit them.

My Father was the pianist in their family, and although I only saw and heard him play by ear, he had studied on that piano while he was a young boy going to school.

Although my Mother was Lutheran, she married my Father in the Temple, since he was Jewish. Kleine Omama was a woman of few words and I believe my parents were married in the Temple at her insistence, even though neither side approved of the marriage.

While looking back at our family's circumstances, my sister and I were never aware of any financial problems. But I now realize the difficulty they must have encountered and I now know how they must have struggled to raise a family in a country defeated by war and suffering an extensive depression. I do not recall Edith and I ever being deprived of any of our needs and wants, although by today's standards, were extremely minimal.

On a few occasions, we had a rented radio. We were never allowed to either listen to the news or read the newspaper for fear that it would destroy our outlook on life. Children growing up during that era were extremely loved, protected, and truly sheltered from outside influence. Our Mother was very protective and attentive, since I do not ever remember leaving our apartment without being accompanied by an adult.

While our parents were very strict, even by standards of the early thirties, my sister, Edith, and I were never deprived of the finer things in life. Education and homework were always our

Mother's number one priority. I well remember being seated at the table with my Mother by my side rewriting papers in my notebook until there were no more mistakes on the paper and the handwriting was perfect. She would not allow erasure marks on any of our homework.

During the week, our Mother would take Edith and I for a leisurely walk to the park, not too distant from our apartment. The park had no recreational equipment, as our children enjoy today, with the exception of a very large sandbox, in which Edith and I were not allowed to play. My Mother was very protective of our health and she feared that other children would throw sand into our eyes.

Edith and I on the way

to the park to play.

If Edith and I behaved well during the week, my parents would give us ten *groschen* (1 penny) and allow us to go to the grocery store on Saturday, located on the first floor of our apartment complex, and purchase a banana. That was a real treat, realizing today that I probably consume on the average of one or two bananas daily.

On Saturdays, we usually attended the opera since movie theaters were generally a no-no. On rare occasions, I attended services at the Temple with my Father, and I recall men seated on one side and women on the other side of the Temple. Although we did not attend on a regular basis, our paternal Jewish Grandmother, Kleine Omama, took Edith and I to Mass at the *Dolfuss Kirche* (church) which was only a few blocks from our apartment. My Mother, being of the Lutheran religion, never took us to a Lutheran service or any other religious one, as I remember, but never objected for Edith and I going to a Catholic Church. Although as I grew up, never thinking about people's different religious persuasion, we always celebrated Christmas and Easter, even though my Father was Jewish.

Although I believe everyone we knew was Catholic in this predominantly Catholic country, religion played an important part in our lives. We never judged others by their religious affiliation. I had attended Sabbath services at the Temple with my Dad on Saturdays to the point where I was able to say some prayers in

Hebrew. By attending mass at the Catholic Church with Kleine Omama, it certainly gave me a broader view of different religions.

I did not know of religious prejudices until Hitler invaded Austria and attempted to annihilate everyone of Jewish faith. Once in a great while, my parents would take us downtown to the business section of Vienna on the *Mariahilfer Strasse* (street) to visit *Gerngross*, which was, and still is, the *Marshall Field* or *Macy's* of Vienna. My parents would always buy Edith and me the finest clothes, and when appropriate, matching outfits.

Edith and I at Schoenbrunn.

It must be realized that ownership of an automobile was a rarity, and of course, we did not own one. We usually walked to wherever we needed to go, and occasionally we would take a trolley to the foot of the mountains surrounding Vienna. We would then walk up the mountain as far as my parents thought that we were able to go, in order to return back home at a decent hour.

On special occasions, we would visit our Aunt Putzi, our Mother's sister, where we were allowed to play with our cousins Freddy, Jutta, and Gusti.

From left to right, Ossie, Edith, Freddy, and Jutta, our cousins, as toddlers in Vienna.

As I remember, summer was always my favorite time during my youth. Our Father sent my Mother, Edith and I to a farm, not too distant from Vienna. I do not recall the farmer's name, but readily remember the farmer scrubbing his limited herd of pigs on a daily basis. His family also raised goats, chickens, and geese. Edith always tried to pick up the baby geese, while the male goose always chased her and pecked her in the calf. Although staying on a farm does not sound very exciting, I loved every moment.

I spent my summers on a farm outside Vienna.

On the farm, I am on the right with
my Mother. Edith is petting the pigs.

When not vacationing on the farm, our parents took us to the Danube River, where we owned a small family cottage. Our parents, both of whom were excellent swimmers, taught Edith and I how to swim. I was always fearful to place my head under water, and even today, although I am a good swimmer, I have not mastered how not to breathe under water.

As you can surmise, my first ten years were mostly fun-filled by my standard of life. However, this would traumatically change in the mid thirties.

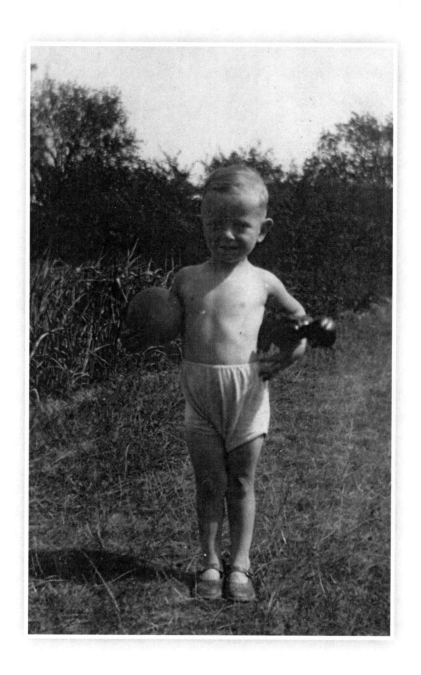

Holding my favorite toys as a toddler.

As I reminisce, it almost seems unbelievable that I grew up without enjoying or remembering friends or playmates. My childhood revolved around my family, our visits to our cousins, and sometimes, a visit to my parents' friends, the Bayer's, who had two daughters, one a few years older than Edith and I, and the other somewhat younger.

My Mother and Edith and I.

My Father and Edith and I.

Once or twice a year, my Father's dad would take me to *Schoenbrunn,* the palace of the former *Kaiser.* I recall I always had to wear a hat, gloves, and carry a cane, since my Grandfather believed it was important to him and members of his family to uphold upper crust appearance. Although I was thrilled when I was told to go with my Grandfather, I do not recall having what a child would perceive as a "fun" time.

Edith and I on one of our outings with our Opapa.

All recreational activities, or excursions, were limited strictly to weekends, since school and homework were the number one priorities during the week. There was no T.V., no computers, no electronic games, no sport activities, only limited radio listening. After school was limited to studying, reading, or going to the park with our parents.

Sports, as we grew up, was something not promoted by schools, the community, clubs, or organizations. It was only available to children whose parents could afford them. Edith and I had the good fortune of learning how to ice skate on one of the only two skating rinks in Vienna, the *Eislauferein* and the more sophisticated *Engelplatz*.

Winter in Vienna

Since my Father played ice hockey for a Viennese team and my Mother was an outstanding skater, she took us at least once a week to the exclusive *Engelplatz* where she taught Edith and I how to skate. I remember vividly that on some occasions, half the rink was roped off to allow a young, future Olympic star, by the name of Sonya Henie, to practice and prepare herself for the Olympics. Of course at that time, none of us realized the fame she would achieve.

Although our Mother could not ski, she taught Edith and I by pushing us from the top of a hill with our Father catching us at the bottom, if we didn't fall first.

Teaching us how to ride a bicycle on weekends was a similar experience with one of our parents standing in the middle of the block on my Grandmother's seldom traveled street, *Die Bein Gasse* (The Bone Street), and the other parent about a hundred and fifty feet away attempting to catch us prior to falling. I do not remember how I faired, but I do recall Edith running into a large window pane in an adjacent store front. Edith and I were only ten and nine years of age at the time. My parents rented a bike on which to train us.

Our Father was proficient in all these activities, and although our Mother was not, (with the exception of skating), it was she who promoted and pushed us to the point of excellence in all these activities.

My parents were very strict disciplinarians. I remember one day when my parents were out. Grosse Omama was working in the kitchen. My sister Edith looked out our apartment window from the second floor. Eyeing my parents coming down the walk, she turned to me and said, "Wouldn't it be funny if you hid under the bed and I told them that you fell out the window?" Always listening to my older sister, I agreed and did what she had suggested.

When my parents entered our apartment, they saw Edith and asked, "Where's Ossie?" Edith responded that I had just fallen out the window. I remember hearing my Mother scream and I reacted by coming out from under the bed and telling them that I was okay. I thought that they would be relieved that I had not fallen out the window and would surely find this event rather humorous.

Instead my Father whipped me and asked, "Why did you do such a thing?" I responded with, "Edith told me to and I listen to her." I received another whipping for being so dumb for listening to her!

Lying to my parents was also not an option in my family. One school day, Edith brought her report card home to show my parents. Upon my arrival at home, they asked me for my report card. I remember receiving a poor mark in one of my subjects and I was ashamed. Not wanting to show them for fear of disappointment, I told them I had not received it yet.

The next day I had given them the same excuse. So the day after that my parents went to school to ask the teacher for my report card. Being very naive and not experienced in hiding, my parents found the card in my desk.

Upon their return home my Father disciplined me by making me kneel on a bamboo stick used for beating rugs. My Mother would come into the room and tell me to please apologize for lying to them. I don't recall how long I knelt on the stick, but it seemed like hours. I finally apologized to my Father. I remember how painful the experience was, for I had indentations on my knees for a very long time. That experience taught me never to lie again!

CHAPTER 2
FEARFUL FLIGHT

Although I was just four and a half years of age at the beginning of the 1930's, unbelievably it was this decade that I
remember most vividly than any other. It was a decade with a
traumatic impact on my family and millions of others. I vividly
remember the assassination of Engelbert Dollfuss, Chancellor of
Austria, and the attempted revolution in Vienna, which prevented
us from visiting our cousins, which we had visited periodically.

I was never, however, aware, at that young age, that we were
also living in the midst of a depression.

We never questioned the meals prepared for us by our
Grandmother. She cooked for us daily since my Mother did not
know how to cook. Every Sunday my Grosse Omama prepared a
goose, which was the only meat we saw all week. It gave us enough
grease to allow us to have goose grease sandwiches for every
school day. During the week we were given all the potatoes with

cottage cheese we could eat and on Fridays, our Grandmother usually prepared carp for our main meal. On Saturday we were given ten *groschen* to buy a banana as a reward for behaving well all week. On special occasions, our parents would take my sister and I to an ice cream parlor for an ice cream cone. Compared to today's available food, our meals were very limited, but we enjoyed everything placed in front of us without complaints.

Our lives were consumed with school and our leisure time involved individual sports and my hobby of collecting stamps.

Although Vienna was in the middle of a political turmoil and minor revolution, Edith and I were spared from much of the news since we did not own a radio and were never allowed to read a newspaper. Both of us continued our rigid school studies and our individual seasonal sport activities until 1938.

I watched my Father's drawn face when he spoke of the Germans or used the word "Nazi". Not until April of 1938, did I realize what fear really meant. That was the fateful day on which Hitler's troops marched into Vienna.

The excitement of watching troops and monstrous guns moving and marching past our apartment complex towards the center of Vienna, made my sister and me rush to our side street apartment windows. To my shock and dismay, our parents pulled us away from the windows and would only allow us to peek through the sheer curtains, so as not to be seen. At the time I did not realize that most every window on the street except ours, displayed the Nazi flag with the *Swastika* (crooked cross). Little did I realize that my parents did not want us recognized looking out a window not displaying the flag.

That was the first time I truly felt fear. I had certainly been scared of my parents, or my teacher about not doing homework, or any such infractions, but never had I experienced what was true fear from the outside and the unknown.

Edith and I continued to go to school while my Father continued to go to work. As a child, I did not realize any changes were taking place, other than seeing many SS (black shirt troops) and SA (brown shirt troops), which were the dreaded enforcers of Nazi Germany. My Mother informed us never to mention that our Dad was Jewish for fear of being arrested and sent to a concentration camp. Our Mother, being Lutheran and of German descent through her parents, blue eyed and blonde, was readily accepted by the Germans, with their Nazi philosophy, considered "true Arian".

Prior to the Nazi occupation of Austria, Austrian patriots painted the *Kruken Kreuz*, Austria's cross, on many of the city's sidewalks. German occupation considered this an outrageous act. As punishment, they forced Jewish women in their expensive minks and other fine clothes, to scrub the sidewalks with lime while the SA and the Jewish hating public would spray them with lime and other harmful chemicals. Although our Mother tried to shield us from seeing these cruel events, it was unavoidable. I never realized that shortly thereafter, they would all be sent to concentration camps to be annihilated.

Although being shocked by these occurrences, I did not realize what impact the Nazis would have on my family. Jealousies and enviousness was as prevalent in 1938 as it is today and it was not very long that it was reported by someone to the Nazi authorities that our Dad was Jewish. The company my Dad managed was owned by Jews, who secretly fled the country soon after Austria's occupation. Although the SA took over the company, my Dad continued to manage it, since they did not know how. If they suspected my Dad of being Jewish, they certainly did not indicate it.

During the month of May, my Father came home early from work and had a heated discussion with my Mother. Although I did not hear the entire conversation, I learned that they had arrested Fritz, my Dad's brother and sent him to a concentration camp. My Mother did not know which one, since that was never made public. The SA took over their manufacturing company and confined my widowed Grandmother to her apartment. At the time I thought she was rather elderly, although she was only in her sixties.

The following morning, my Mother told me that I would not have to go to school that day, but that I must accompany my

Dad wherever he went, and I was never to let go of his hand, no matter what would happen. I do not recall what I possibly said, but I vividly recall my Mother saying to me that no matter what happens or no matter what my Dad says, I am not to let go of his hand, since he would be sent to a concentration camp and killed if I did. Fear truly set in then, although at the age of eleven, little did I understand the great danger.

Vienna was a huge metropolis, and my Father, not wanting to be spotted on a bus or trolley car, informed me that we would have to walk or sometimes even run to wherever he needed to go. I know I did not ask any questions. I only remember being scared about what Mom told me.

We walked to the *Argentine Embassy* where we encountered a long line of people. My Father seemed to know several of them, and although I clutched his hand standing close to him, I could not hear what they said. They all looked so serious and only whispered. I remember standing in line into the early afternoon, when a gentleman said something to my Dad and we immediately left the waiting line. Later I learned all who stayed in line at the *Argentine Embassy* were arrested.

We walked away hurriedly going down side streets and staying away from any busy arteries. We never stopped to eat, and I was fearful to ask my Dad to stop. I don't believe we ever said anything to each other, only grasping each other's hand, with my Dad's grip sometimes being very strong, when he apparently noticed or saw something that would endanger us. Late that night my Father called someone from a public phone, since we had no phone, and I was greatly distressed since I had to let go of my Father's hand. We continued to walk up and down various streets and I only hoped Dad would not tell my Mother that I let go of his hand, for fear of punishment.

Sometime around midnight, a taxi pulled alongside of us, someone jumped out and pushed my Father into the taxi, while pulling me away. Not until weeks later did I realize the taxi driver was my Uncle August Pospichal, my Mother's brother-in-law, who came to hide my Father.

CHAPTER 3
LAST YEAR IN AUSTRIA

Shortly after my Father went into hiding at Aunt Putzi's apartment, my Mother informed us that Edith and I were to go to a different school. My memory is somewhat vague as to how long we attended this segregated school, which was created by the Nazis to be attended by children from Jewish parents and for children from families who the Nazis wished to annihilate or discriminate against. Little did we realize that most of those children would be sent to concentration camps.

My Father and Mother and Edith and
I in happier times before my Father went into hiding.

My earlier school days. I am on the end in the first row on the right.
My teacher, Mr. Novak, is in the middle.

Our good fortune of survival was our Mother's "Arian" background, her proud and sometimes arrogant and belligerent attitude, which I believe was accepted only by the Nazis. She was an elegantly dressed, attractive, blonde woman in her late thirties.

We were constantly told that if questioned or asked by anyone about our Father's whereabouts, we were to say that we had not seen him and believed he was sent to a concentration camp. I think back many times in amazement, that our Mother entrusted her twelve and thirteen year old children with the knowledge of my Dad's hiding place, without her fearing that we might inadvertently reveal it.

My courageous Mother,

Edith and I.

We never visited my Dad the many months he remained in hiding. While Edith and I attended school, my Mother went to the various consulates which were willing to issue people a visa number wishing to leave Austria. Low visa numbers were the most desirable, since they allowed you to leave the country the quickest, but were the most difficult to obtain. Many countries, such as Argentina, Ireland, Italy, and countries on other continents, were Nazi sympathizers, and informed the Nazi authorities the moment you left their embassies to be arrested and sent to concentration camps.

My parents had a long time friend, who had played ice hockey with my Father. He, I know, assisted her to acquire a visa to allow us to get to Switzerland, although I don't believe my Mother ever told him of my Father's hiding place.

My Mother had secured a visa for the four of us for China, and although I surmised she did not want to go there, we were in such a desperate situation to leave the country. I know she expressed delight that she had acquired all necessary papers for us to leave for China through Switzerland. While making preparations of how to bring my Dad out of hiding and leave the country, she informed Edith and I that my Uncle Fritz was released from the concentration camp. Since no Jew, to my knowledge, was ever released alive from a concentration camp, I am certain that through my Mother's effort and "Arian" connection, she obtained his release. I remember he had three days to leave the country or be sent back to *Dachau*. Uncle Fritz stayed with us during that time period, hiding under the bed like an animal anytime we heard a knock on the door. I recall when we came home from school several days later, my Mother told us that Fritz left the country.

Although prior to the occupation of Austria, my Mother and Kleine Omama visited infrequently. After the occupation my Mother visited her on a daily basis, to make certain she would not be taken by the Nazis to a concentration camp. As I reminisce, I stand in awe of my Mother for accomplishing the almost impossible.

Finally one day, my Father came home and we were informed we were to tell everyone that we were leaving for Switzerland on a three day holiday. My aunt had shaven my Father's head, so as to make it appear he had been in a concentration camp. The train station, *Westbahnhof*, was not too distant from our apartment. Our uncle, August Pospichal, (my Mother's brother-in-law, who had hidden our Dad) took us to the train station in his taxi. There were no emotional goodbyes, since my parents made it appear as a weekend outing.

```
B.H.No.Otto 9000/1              K I N D E R:
      Fritz7986
        Mama 18604           Edith and Oswald
   Visa-Nummern.             arrived in London
Otto   628  7/15 40.         May24th.1939
Mimi   783  7/17 40.            1o'cl.Croydon Airpt
Diti   785  7/17 40.
Ossy   784  7/17 40.
Ida    13Oct7/25 40.

   Pass-Nummern.
Otto 77453 1/19.39.
Mimi 77454 1/18.39.
Diti L18640 7/16.40.
Ossy 1800N 23/39.40.
Mama 183938 7/8.39.
```

```
Wien Abf.So.19.3.39      New York:Ank.So.25.8.40
       3.30 Westbhf.        Pennsylv.Stat.11Uhrm.
Zuerich Ank.6h20.3.39    Abf.3.12.40 Dienstag
Evang.Toechterheim       Greyhoundstat.12.45
   Lutherstrasse 12.     Chicago: Ank.4.12.40
Abf.v.Flugplatz Duesen    5 Uhr nahm.
dorf Mo.27.3.39 1Uhr
ParisFlugplatz 3UhrAnk
Abf. 4.30 n.London

London:Ank.6Uhr27.3,39
Abf.16.Aug.1940 n.USA.
   9Uhr v.Euston Stat
Liverpool  16.8.1940

Ank. 1 Uhr
Abf. 8Uhrabs.auf
   Duchess of Athøll
Montreal Ank.24.8.40
```

A list of our visa numbers and destinations written in 1939.

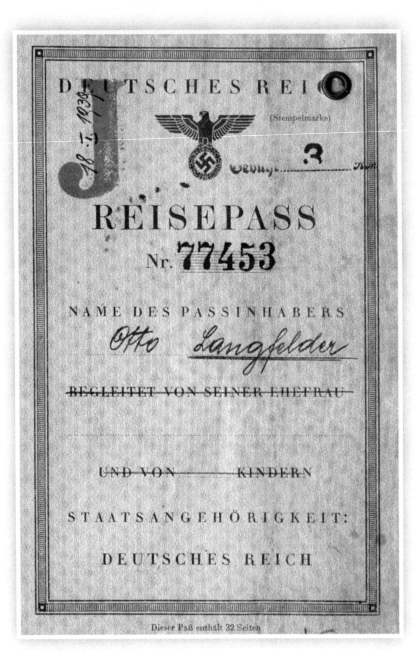

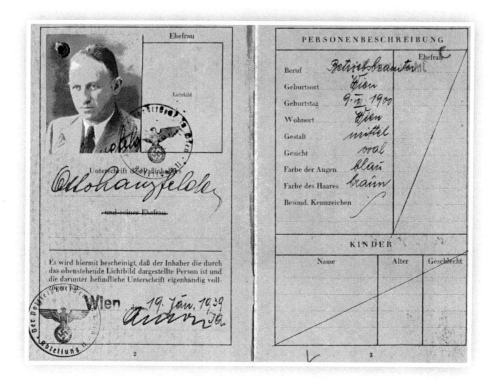

My Father's passport to leave Austria.
It was stamped with a red "J" for Jew.

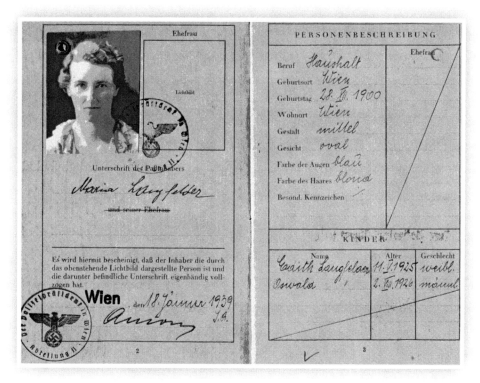

My Mother's passport to leave Austria.
Even though she was Lutheran, her
passport was also marked with a
red "J" for Jew.

I still recall arriving at the Swiss border late at night. The train had stopped and the SS came through the train questioning some passengers, taking some from the train, looking at everyone's papers and passports. When they came to us, my Dad opened his satchel containing our clothes. They ordered all valuables to be turned over to them. As a stamp collector, I had taken a small booklet of my favorite stamps which they took from me. I have never forgotten that, which at the time, was a very devastating ordeal for me. Within seconds, they grabbed my mother and carted her away. Our passports displayed a large, red "J" for Jew and apparently when they recognized my Mother's "Arian" appearance, they were infuriated with her for marrying a Jew. My Father did not utter a word, for fear of being sent away.

It seemed like an eternity before my Mother returned. She had been stripped and searched, and God knows what, since she never would speak of it. This dignified lady, I know, felt violated and disgraced. As my Mother sat down, we saw the Nazis leave the train and we rolled slowly across the border. Upon stopping again, Swiss border guards boarded the train and I can still hear the voices as they looked at our passports, *"Gruess Gott!"* (Greet God!) and *"Wie Geht es Ihnen?"* (How are you?). Our parents cried and laughed, and then Edith and I did the same. Because of our parents, we were not to understand the dangers and emotions, which we had been encountering for future years.

Not until we arrived in the *Aich Hotel* were Edith and I told that our parents were going to England, while leaving us in foster homes in Switzerland. Edith and I had no visas for any other country, but only possessed a sixty to ninety day visiting permit to Switzerland. While Edith stayed in Zurich with a doctor's family, I was taken to the mountains by a postman to stay with a lady on her farm. Although my guardian was extremely good to me, I was a homesick, ungrateful twelve year old who wanted to return to my friends, relatives, and belongings in Vienna.

My passport picture and
Identification to leave Austria.

I longed for my earlier days.

CHAPTER 4
ENGLAND

Our sixty to ninety day visiting permit was rapidly expiring. Living in the mountains made communications with the outside world very limited. Telephone service in homes was almost unheard of and the remote area where we lived only had contact once a week with a postman.

Although I wanted to be reunited with my parents and sister, deep within me, I hoped that our visiting permit to Switzerland would expire prior to my parents acquiring a visa for Edith and me to go to England. I was a very homesick, young boy, and my thoughts were always to return home to Vienna.

The year was 1939 when my foster mother informed me that I was to meet my sister in Zurich. Although I was treated extremely well by everyone with whom I became associated, I did not have a tearful departure, but rather one that was pretty much emotionless. The mailman took me to Zurich on his motorcycle. I recall the gravel roads were rather steep and it took well over an hour to arrive at our destination. My memory is very hazy at this point, but I remember Edith's temporary guardians taking us to the airport.

Flying in the late thirties was reserved for the military and the very rich. Since Switzerland is a landlocked country and Edith and I had no visas to enter any other country, our only option was to fly. We were fortunate that our parents found sponsors to pay for our trip. Although the plane appeared very large to me, by comparison to today's planes, it was about the size of a commuter plane. Never having flown before, the turbulence we encountered made me very airsick. A little girl who sat directly behind me, periodically hit me on the head. I don't remember if I complained to anyone, but I know it exasperated my ill feeling.

The plane on which we flew from Zurich to
Croyden, London on May 24, 1939.

After what seemed like an eternity, we landed at *Croyden Airport* near London. The minute we left the plane, Edith and I saw our parents standing on the observation deck of the airport. It was certainly a happy experience, and as of that moment, it seemed as if only the present counted, no thoughts of the past or the future. As we passed through the gates, we encountered a tremendously new experience. Until we could embrace our parents, we were unable to communicate, since we spoke no English and the British refused to speak German.

The shock of this experience lasted only a few seconds. I cannot remember how we traveled to the place where my parents resided, but I do recall Uncle Fritz welcoming us upon our arrival. He was certainly a pleasant sight, and after many months, if only for a short period of time, I actually recall being happy. I had not realized that where my parents actually had been living, was the home of a wealthy, British family who employed my Mother as their maid and my Father as their butler in return for sponsoring our family.

My Uncle Fritz, on the left, visiting my family in London, England,

at the home of our sponsor, second from left.

My family and I in London, England.

After spending a couple of days with our parents, we were told that Edith and I had to go to boarding schools and would no longer be allowed to stay at the family mansion. Soon thereafter, the family bought me clothes, such as a school uniform, gray shorts, a red and green blazer, and a red and green cap, (a cap which I still have in my possession). I was then taken to the school which I was to attend: *St. Aloysius College* in Highgate, London. I remember my Father being with me when I arrived at the school, where for the first time, we met Brother Cornelius Reed, who was to be my tutor. The school at that time was well over a hundred years old. The interior was dark and very dreary to me.

In London, England wearing my school uniform.

On the streets of London, England.

Again I felt anguished as my Father left me, not knowing when I might see him again. I was unable to communicate since no one spoke German, whether intentional or by design. Once more I was in a very frightening situation since my stubbornness over-shadowed my good sense, as I rebelled against learning English. Brother Cornelius' patience, however, won me out as he taught me English by pointing and stating the item's name, while I stated it in German. I struggled in daytime while fretting at night time.

After several months at Highgate, Great Britain declared war on Germany, and soon thereafter, the bombardments of London began. We would be informed that we would be evacuated to a small community named Wisbech, well distant from London. I wasn't sure what that meant, except I knew that, again, I would be separated from my parents for a long period of time. It was not a happy time for me, and as we would say today, "I was not a happy camper." We took a train to Wisbech and with my little knowledge of English, I thought we were being sent to another boarding school.

As we arrived in Wisbech, Brother Cornelius did inform me in German that we were to be placed in private residences for the duration of the war, the length which none could predict. The village had a population of about 1,500. Brother Cornelius marched with about fifty students down the middle of the street of a residential area. He would stop at a house and ask the occupants how many boys they would house for the duration of the war. Most would take two or three students. I am certain Brother Cornelius described various students, as it appeared to me that the people would point to the ones they wanted to care for.

Brother Cornelius who taught me with his patience, guidance and understanding.

It was starting to get dark when the only boy remaining to be taken in by someone was me. I never thought much about being the last boy to find housing until later in life when I learned the British's reluctance to accept someone who was unable to speak or understand English.

The family who agreed to house me for the duration of the war was an elderly couple, Mr. and Mrs. Johnson. My stay with them lasted about eighteen months. I remember the Johnson's lived on a tiny farm and raised rabbits. Even though food was rationed during this time, we ate rabbit every day. Sometimes, their older daughter, who was in her thirties, would take me to town to the theater, and on Fridays, we would eat fish and chips instead of rabbit. To this day I have not eaten rabbit again!

My dear parents!

I am very happy here. Here is it very naic. The person is very good to me. I got to eat what I like. I got 7 Penni from Missis Johnson. We have here naic mother. We have a naic house and a naic small cat. We have many trees with apples, pairs and plums. We have two gardens. I have not many things here. Two coats 2 trosers and the undercloths. I have not my books to lern here. I Next week we must go to the school. This is fine. Missis and Mister Johnson are very good to me. I can have what I wont. When a person go out must have a gasmask. What to you doing every time? Have you recived my card? This here is a naic place. I write this letter not with a dictionary. I understand english very well. I have a naic room. A bic bed 3 chairs and a washstand chist of drawers. I can go out every days with other boys there are ten living on this road. I go in the afternoon out with brother and with other boys. I ride yesterday a bicigcle to the garden. When you write me a letter you can write me in english. I dont not more for to-day I finisht my letter.

The best gretting and kiss from your

Osry

This is my address.

*Oswald Langfelder % Missis Johnson
72 Leverangton Road, Wisbech.*

*One of the letters I wrote to my parents when
I stayed with the Johnson's.*

CHAPTER 5
UNITED STATES

Entering the United States was not an easy task. Our family entered the United States on a temporary visa, through Canada. In those days, one could only come to the United States if you had a sponsor who would guarantee that they would support your needs. Your sponsor needed to be willing to support you because you could not be a financial burden on the government.

My Immigration visa.

Our parents, Edith and I left London, England by train for Liverpool, where upon we were to leave for the United States. Upon our arrival we boarded our ship, the *Duchess of Atholl*, which was filled with hundreds of children and a few elderly guardians who were being evacuated to Canada for the duration of the war.

In August 1940, our ship embarked from Liverpool, England for Quebec, Canada. The trip across the ocean seemed to be never ending as I was extremely seasick. The trip took four times longer as a normal trip of a few days. In order to avoid a German U-boat attack, our ship had a destroyer escort which zigzagged across the Atlantic. Of course the children on board, including my sister and I, were never made aware of the situation. Since land was never visible, we were unaware of the ship's maneuvers.

During my younger years, I was a sleepwalker, which normally is not harmful to the individual. However, on this ship, it could have been a catastrophe. So after my first venture of sleep walking onto the deck during the night, my parents always made certain that our cabin door was locked when we went to sleep.

When we finally saw land, I remember everyone on the ship cheered. I don't know if I was happy because we had avoided a U-boat attack or because we were finally going to land. I was certainly glad that I was fortunate to be with my family, since most of the other children left their dear ones in England, not know-ing when or if they would see them again. I have always been a worrier, (to which my wife could certainly testify), as my next thoughts and fears on land was what to expect and anticipate.

I recall that on that day we disembarked, the weather was somewhat dreary, but I was so happy to be able to put my feet on solid ground that nothing else really mattered. I do not recall if we stayed overnight in Montreal or if we took a train to New York immediately after disembarking.

We arrived in New York City on Sunday, August 26, 1940. Arriving in New York was like a fairy tale to me - the skyscrapers, the lights, the thousands of people - was something that will always be etched in my memories. My "Uncle Paul", my Father's cousin, met us and escorted us to a somewhat dingy, but clean apartment on 72nd Street. My "Uncle" had been more fortunate than most refugees, by escaping from Austria just prior to Hitler's takeover, thereby bringing his valuables and other belongings with him.

I vividly recall going to a store close to *Time's Square* which displayed a four foot by four foot cube of butter in a huge glass case near the entrance of the store. My eyes must have bulged out, since coming from England, where everything was rationed and where we hardly had any opportunity to even see butter. Food was very limited in England since the German U-boats blockaded that island. No one in this country could ever visual-ize how my family and I felt seeing all the food displayed, as you see in supermarkets today. We never knew that stories of this magnitude existed. We had no idea how long we would be in New York, although I hoped we would stay for the duration of the war in Europe, so we could return home as soon as the war ended. Little did I realize that my parents never intended to return, and that the USA would become our permanent home.

Our parents enrolled Edith and me in *Blessed Sacrament Grade School* on 72nd Street, not too distant from our apartment. (The school is still there today.) Although boys and girls attended classes in the same facility, the classrooms were not coed. Considering that Edith and I were still learning English, we both did extremely well, although I was just a very reluctant student. I always felt it would not be long before I could return home, which was always my greatest yearning.

I had studied English in England for one and a half years, but I was not prepared to understand English in New York City. I felt like I was starting all over again to learn the language.

"Uncle Paul" was successful in finding my Father a job in Chicago, Illinois for an oil company. In those days, there were many manufacturing companies with heavy machines. Huge belts were detrimental in running the equipment and oil lubricants were in high demand.

So one day, upon arriving home from school, our parents informed Edith and I that we would be moving to Chicago, since my Father found a job there. I, for one, did not have any idea where Chicago was located, and I was totally decimated that it was almost another thousand miles from my Vienna.

Left to right,
Edith, Kleine Omama, my Father and me in upstate New York.
It was the first time I had seen my Grandmother since I left Austria.

CHAPTER 6
SPRINGFIELD, OUR NEW HOME

After our move to Chicago, I remember sitting around the kitchen table. Not knowing the size of the State of Illinois, my parents put a map on the kitchen table, figuring they could pick a city which was centrally located. Because we did not own a vehicle, my parents surmised that my Father could walk to wherever he could to sell the oil if we were centrally located. My Mother closed her eyes and pointed to the map - Springfield was our destination.

When we settled in Springfield, at the time, there were many manufacturing businesses: *Allis-Chambers, Pillsbury, Sangamo Electric, Hobbs.* On the first day of my Father's job, he walked to *Illinois Soy Products.* The owner bought one quart of oil from my Father because he was so impressed that my Father, an immigrant, would walk five miles to the company to make a living. That day, my Father walked another five miles home and my Mother fixed a full course meal to celebrate his success. I know I received my dedicated work ethics from my Father and determined drive from my Mother.

Arriving in Springfield, Illinois for me was a total mental disaster. I could not believe that I was being banished to such a small community, around 58,000, in the midst of hundreds of farms!

My Father, receiving financial and other support from the congregation of the Temple on South Fourth Street, moved us into an apartment in the 900 block of North Third Street. Since we had no personal possessions, other than our clothes, moving never appeared to be a logistical problem.

Mom was very devastated. This was not a neighborhood of her choosing or status, nor did she appreciate a dingy apartment on the second floor. Although we had no money and the Temple paid for everything, we soon moved to a beautiful first story apartment across from *McClernand School*, which my Mother had picked out. I never saw the amount of the rent, since my parents never discussed money in front of us. It must have been a tidy amount, since I recall my Mother saying she did not care how much it costs, since she never lived in a dump and was not going to allow her children to live in one, even if someone else had to pay for it.

My Mother loved cats and kept one most her life. Upon her arrival in Springfield, she found a black cat for which she purchased a leash. I vividly recall the first Friday night we walked downtown with the cat on a leash. Downtown businesses were open on Friday nights and hundreds of people were looking and shopping. Our Father told Edith and I not to speak unless it was in English, for fear we would be ostracized of being overheard speaking German. I, of course, wore my *Lederhosen*, which was my Austrian style of clothing. I know everyone stared at us not only for walking a cat on the leash, but also for our dress which was certainly not American style.

One day we came home from school and my Mother told us that she had prepared a chicken dinner for us. My Mother did not learn to cook until she was forty years old. Much to our surprise, she served us our dinner. We noticed that there was a lot of liquid with the chicken. We were very surprised that she knew how to make gravy. As she started cutting the chicken we noticed that the inside part of the chicken was still intact, hence the gravy. Since we were laughing at my Mother because she did not clean the inside of the chicken out before cooking it, she punished us by making us eat it anyway.

I joined the Boy Scouts when I came to Springfield. My Scout Masters were Mr. Siebert and Louis LaBonte. I belonged to *Troop 1* and one of my projects was collecting aluminum cans for the war effort.

I was pictured in <u>Boys' Life</u> in 1942.

I am on the bottom right hand corner.

I joined the Scouts when I came to Springfield, because I was a

Scout in England and enjoyed it.

Edith and I enrolled in *Lanphier High School,* where we were made to feel at home by most of the teachers. Edith seemed to be right at home immediately after our arrival, making friends quickly. I had much greater difficulty, since I hardly befriended anyone, with my thoughts usually being on Vienna. Edith and I entered the same second half of the sophomore grade. Edith played the clarinet in the band, while I played the cello in the orchestra. We both took the same subjects, although I do not recall ever being in the same classroom with Edith. While she excelled in drama, it was I who participated in a school play.

I participated in a play as Lord Archibald at Lanphier High School

I am standing on the right.

I am standing on the left with my fellow actors and actresses.

I became the coeditor of the *Lanphier Light,* the school newspaper. This afforded me many opportunities to meet internation-
ally renowned individuals. I was fortunate to interview Colonel
Romulo, President of the Philippines; Prince Otto of Austria,
Pretender of the throne; Ethel Barrymore, one of America's
most famous actresses; Victor Mature, a movie idol of the forties
and fifties; and the Von Trapp Family, of the now world famous
Sound of Music.

Because I was considered teacher's pet for two of my teachers,
Mr. McGann and Mr. Gerald, some of the student body, mainly

the football jocks, disliked me. One day Mr. McGann, our mechanical drawing instructor, assigned me to monitor the class while he left the room. Most of the students in the class were members of the football team and took the class for easy credit. They became somewhat boisterous and noisy. I raised my 110 pound body from Mr. McGann's chair and with my heavily accented voice, asked them to sit down and be quiet. The Saputo twins, the #1 fullbacks in Springfield (and 190 lbs. +), took great offense, charged the desk, and picked me up to give me a whipping just as Mr. McGann entered the room. He asked, I believed for my benefit, who started the fight. As all of us kept quiet, he reprimanded each of us. Since I didn't squeal, however, none of the jocks nor anyone else, ever picked on me again.

I enjoyed attending *Lanphier High School*, although I was only allowed to attend dances if Edith and her girlfriends accompanied me. Since I was rather scrawny, I was never active in sports, and even Mr. Rake, our gym instructor, threw me out of class. He was a very crude, cursing individual whom, I felt, didn't like anyone who spoke to him in a polite manner.

The Japanese attacked Pearl Harbor as I was completing my first semester at *Lanphier*. The war, at first, had a minor impact on the student body, but as we progressed into our senior year, all the young male students, upon reaching the age of seventeen, enlisted in the armed services. Unbeknownst to my parents, with the help of my principal, Mr. Stickney, I also attempted to enlist, but to no avail. Not being a citizen and being under the age of eighteen, I was not accepted. I was very disillusioned and feared the war would end prior to my returning to Europe. As I remained at *Lanphier,* Edith and I graduated together and continued our education at *Springfield Junior College.* While attending *Springfield Junior College,* (now known as *Benedictine University*) I received my draft notice.

CHAPTER 7
DRAFT AND SERVICE

Since most of my high school friends and acquaintances had already left several months before me, I was eager to have been drafted. Although I attempted to enlist, I was not accepted since I was still a citizen of Austria and had not lived long enough in the United States to apply for American citizenship. It should also be noted that Austria was considered friendly to Germany and therefore its' citizens were an enemy to the United States. As a matter of fact, my Father traveled on business throughout Illinois and had to register so as not to leave Springfield without special permission.

Edith and I finally graduated in January 1944 and continued our education at *Springfield Junior College*. After completing my first semester, and an answer to my prayers, I received my draft notice.

Although I was happy to finally be able to enter the Armed Services, my departure was very emotional for my parents, Edith, and me. After only having spent four years together, we again were going to be split up, with a very uncertain future. I was of very small stature, barely weighing 120 pounds when entering the service. My parents, having been very protective, never encouraging physical labor or exertion, made my basic training extremely difficult and my anxiety to rise beyond comprehension.

On this very cold day in January 1945, we boarded the train at Third and Washington for *Fort Sheridan* located by Chicago, Illinois. I remember it was a tearful and very emotional goodbye, even for my well composed Mother. We did not know when or where we might see each other again. I was only eighteen years of age and it seemed to me as if this war had gone on for my entire childhood.

We were inducted in *Fort Sheridan* where we stayed for about a week before being sent to *Fort Sill,* Oklahoma for our basic training. I remember leaving *Fort Sheridan* during a bitter cold wintry day with our heavy, wool, full-length overcoats and wool uniforms. By our clothing issue, we anticipated being transported to a training camp in the northern part of the United States. However, we arrived the following mid morning at *Fort Sill* with the temperature around 90 degrees. We were only allowed to carry our duffle bag and were ordered to wear our coats while marching to our assigned barracks. It was a day I will always remember.

The sixteen week course was strenuous, although we did have some fun times. *Fort Sill,* located close to Lawton, Oklahoma, was in the middle of rattlesnake country. My fellow trainees knew of my fear of snakes, so while we were out on bivouac, (camping out) asleep in our individual pup tents, they hung a dead rattler at the end of my tent. When I woke up the following morning and saw the snake, never realizing it was dead, I shot out the opposite end of the tent, tearing out the stakes which had anchored my tent down.

Being of very small stature, I had great difficulty scaling the high wooden walls during our rigid, training program. On one occasion, they ordered us to drive two and a half ton dump trucks to the middle of this huge pond, stop the engine, restart, and continue. Never having driven before, I apparently flooded the engine and was forced to jump into the water and swim to shore fully dressed. I was never allowed to drive another vehicle during my term in the service. I never realized that almost all eighteen year olds in the United States knew how to drive, but I had never been given that opportunity.

Basic training at Fort Sill, Lawton, Oklahoma.

After completing my basic training at *Fort Sill*, I received my citizenship in Oklahoma City before I could be shipped out. My company was then sent to an undisclosed destination by troop train. Upon arrival, we learned that we were in *Fort Meade*, Maryland, a point of embarkation for the European Theater of War. I was actually in ecstasy, since being sent to Europe meant that I might be able to return to Vienna after the war, whenever that might be.

A few days after arriving at *Fort Meade*, (to which we were confined and not allowed to communicate with anyone from the outside), we packed all our gear for embarkation. I don't know if others were as thrilled as I to be leaving for Europe, but I guess it was extremely important to me to be able to fight the Germans. As the men went single file up the ramp to the ship, I was pulled from the ranks and escorted back to the barracks. It was a fearful episode, since I was told nothing and ordered to stay until further notice.

That evening I was escorted to the mess hall and after finishing my meal, brought back to this huge, empty barracks, which just a few hours before, housed somewhat less than 100 soldiers. I stayed in that vacated barracks a little over two days, never being informed about what was to happen. Having escaped Nazi atrocities without having been harmed certainly made me feel blessed, and now, only four years after coming to this country, I feared what the Americans would do to me.

I was summoned to headquarters, given traveling vouchers, and informed the next day that I would be sent on a civilian train to *Camp Adaire,* Oregon. I was instructed (ordered) not to talk to anyone about my situation or destination. I joined a troop train west of Chicago and when we stopped to refuel, I handed a letter to someone on the platform requesting that they would mail it to my parents for me. Although we were not allowed to communicate, I wanted my parents to know that I was alright and being shipped to these various camps. I don't know whether I was frightened or dismayed, but I only hoped I'd be sent to Alaska and not the South Pacific.

Camp Adaire, Oregon was also a staging area for the various ports of embarkation, besides being a prison camp for Italian captives. We again were under strict orders not to communicate with anyone, being confined to the camp. Interestingly enough, the Italian captives moved freely through the compound and were given passes to go to town.

I was assigned to the 27th Infantry Division. After a few days, we were reissued winter uniforms and marched onto a "Victory" Ship. Having being issued winter uniforms, I felt reassured that we were heading for Alaska, in which direction our ship headed when we first left port. After being aboard only a few days, we realized the ship was taking a different direction. During various maneuvers in an attempt to avoid submarines, we were locked in our quarters, which happened to be water tight compartments. Although the compartments were between seven and eight feet high, we slept on triple-decker canvas cots. I was extremely seasick and our lieutenant allowed me to stay on deck. My sickness was so overwhelming that I did not care where we were being sent, as long as I could set foot on land.

After over two weeks on the ship, we landed on the island of *Mog Mog*, a rest and recreation island for incoming and outgoing ships. *Mog Mog* was a part of the Marshall Islands. To best describe the island is to say that it had maybe twenty palm trees, was as flat as a pancake, about two feet above sea level, and welcoming thousands of American soldiers with cartons of cigarettes and cases of beer or coke for each. After returning to the ship, I became severely ill, as it was diagnosed that I was given green beer to drink, which apparently poisoned my stomach. For the following three days, I remained in the ship's infirmary, and upon my discharge, was again allowed to sleep on the deck for the remainder of our "journey". It was several days later that we were told our destination was Okinawa. We learned that the Marines and infantry had the island under control and we, as members of the field artillery, were replacements for the units which suffered heavy casualties.

As we arrived, the sea was very rough, and because of the height of the waves, the landing crafts on which we were to embark, could not be locked onto the ship. Everyone with their gear and rifles climbed over the railing onto enormous rope nets. We had trained on such nets, but never realized I would actually embark on one. Not being muscular and only weighing about 120 pounds, it was obvious I could not carry all that equipment down the side of the ship without falling at least seventy feet onto the landing craft.

Many things go through your mind at such a desperate moment and although I wish I could remember, I cannot recall the names of the soldiers on either side of me descending on the rope nets. Carrying all their own equipment, one grabbed my duffle bag and one my rifle. After descending several feet, they yelled at me to wait until the waves lifted the landing craft just a few feet below. At that instance they jumped while I hung frozen to the net. By the time I released my hands, the craft was over thirty feet below me, and I luckily fell upon several duffle bags. After all assigned soldiers were in the craft, we took an extremely choppy trip to shore. Upon landing in Okinawa, we waded on shore as we had often seen General Douglas MacArthur do in news reels.

I recall it was dusk and one's thoughts are only on what was next. We were transported to the various units. Several others and I were assigned to *155 Howitzer Company*. Only two seasoned veterans had survived. They looked at us *Green Hornes* with some dismay and the sadness and exhaustion was very visible in their faces. No one spoke and it was obvious we had to learn by observing and watching these vets. It was a terrifying experience, although you were with many soldiers who were just as terrified. C-rations were distributed, and as these veterans opened their C-ration cans, they dumped their contents into their helmets and heated them over an open fire. We all followed suit, none of us uttering a word. We had learned in boot camp how to shoot and how to fight, but now we had to learn how to survive. It was a lonely feeling, an indescribable feeling.

I served in the army from
January 1945 – December 1946.
I am in Japan with Don Tarulli.

In Japan with my

fellow soldiers.

I am standing second

from right.

The night we landed, Okinawa was a sea of mud. We had no sleeping quarters and the only tent available was occupied by the surviving two veterans. Although it wasn't discussed, I knew that none of us recruits would ever think of depriving them of the cots and tent, which they so richly deserved. By nightfall we had all spread our ponchos on the muddy ground and gone to sleep. I know I prayed selfishly that night, wishing that the war would be soon over. I know I cried, but there was no one to seek comfort in my assignment as *forward observer* was not in demand any longer. The island was now secure, with the exception of some Japanese hiding in caves and coming out at night to attack the sleeping troops. Since the *Howitzers* were only used sporadically, the troops assigned to them became the infantry ordered to annihilate the Japanese in the caves. A few weeks after our arrival, Japan surrendered and we were informed, that we, who were assigned to the 27th infantry division, would fly into Japan as the first occupational troops.

In Japan during my tour of duty.

CHAPTER 8
JAPAN

We landed at *Atsugi Airfield*, located between Yokohama and Tokyo, Japan and transported by train to a camp near Tokyo. Now assigned to the 77th Infantry Division, we were instructed not to go to Tokyo until the First Calvary Division arrived, since that was General MacArthur's pride and he wanted them in Tokyo first. After a couple of days waiting for the General and his troops to arrive, we marched in force into Tokyo, watching the General occupy the *Daichi Building* and becoming the ruler of Japan.

I was amazed at the beauty of Tokyo and the politeness of the few Japanese with whom we came in contact. Although we occupied the country of a devout enemy, I think none of us were fearful of what might or could have happened. Our company's stay in Tokyo was to be very short lived and our platoon was ordered to occupy an army camp in Wakamatsu, a community of about 80,000 in the middle of Honshu Island. We did not know what to expect, as I am certain our army brass did likewise. All of us carried carbines, with our ranking officer, a sergeant, carrying a pistol. We all had been issued two cartridges of bullets, certainly hoping the use of which would never be necessary.

Our first picture in Japan after our occupation.
The woman is the photographer's wife. I am standing behind her.

Twelve of us rode in three jeeps approximately 150 miles north of Tokyo. We drove through numerous villages where we saw very few Japanese. Every house and building had been boarded for fear of the Americans. Signs designating the names of communities had been removed so we would not know where we were. Little did they know that we could not read Japanese anyway.

After driving well over six hours, we arrived at what we believed to be Wakamatsu, Japan. I recall it was late afternoon, and as we drove through the community with the boarded up buildings, I remember seeing no more than three people on the streets. Although our sergeant had a city map, I will never know how he located the army camp. I can still see the twelve of us jump out of our jeeps, load our carbines, and watch one of the men approach an enormous, wooden gate of what resembled a stockade of the "Cowboy-Indian Era". As he pounded, the gate was opened and the twelve of us marched into the parade grounds facing a Japanese Company of over 250 soldiers.

We had not been instructed as what to do in this situation, but apparently did not appear dumbfounded by the Japanese. Their commanding officer spoke little English, said they were surrendering, stacked all their various weapons neatly on the parade grounds, and then marched with his troops out of camp. Their discipline astonished us all, since we were no match had they resisted us. As we surveyed their living quarters, we quickly learned that they were flea infested and we opted to sleep on the parade grounds until the remainder of our company arrived.

After spending a few months in Wakamatsu, I was ordered to join another company located in Sapporo, Japan. Sapporo was a similar sized community located on Hokkaido, the northern most island of Japan. I was ordered by myself to go by train to the northern tip of Honshu Island and then by boat to Hakodate, where I was picked up by jeep and driven to Sapporo. It was bitter cold with snow drifts as deep as ten feet.

Regimental headquarters in Sapporo.

My assignment was in communications as a radio operator. Since traveling was very difficult due to the severe winter conditions, all of us were authorized to use horses from the stables for transportation purposes.

Sleeping quarters in our barracks in Sapporo.
I am seated second from the right.

After serving several weeks in Hokkaido, I was again transferred to a camp not too distant from Yokohama. I was part of a cadre in charge of a company of black soldiers. At that time, the army was still segregated with white officers and noncommissioned officers in charge of black troops. Although the cadre was authorized to carry loaded weapons, the black troops were not. In late September 1946, I was ordered to return home to be discharged. This trip, although I became seasick, was one of enjoyment since we were allowed to sleep and eat when and wherever we felt like it.

We landed in Seattle, Washington and although we had the opportunity to be discharged, for some reason, I was unable to contact my parents. Upon arriving by train in Springfield, I took a taxi to the house they had bought during my absence, which I had never seen. I surmised that my army checks that had been sent to my parents, were being used as a down payment for their house on North Illinois Street. To my dismay, I cannot recall our reunion, although it must have been very emotional.

I know coming back to Springfield, Illinois was like a new beginning. I was twenty years old and really did not know many people. My best friend, Allen Williams, had been killed during the last few days of the war in Europe and the very few young people I remembered, were either away at school or had new friends.

Although most veterans joined the *52:20 Club*, receiving $20 for 52 weeks of unemployment, I went to work within a week of coming home at *Arch Wilson Clothing Store* while waiting to enroll at *Springfield Junior College* in January of 1947.

I had a great time at *Springfield Junior College*, graduating in May 1948, and then entering *Purdue University*. Although I had dated different girls, none ever appealed to my parents and it was actually a relief to attend school away from Springfield. Although I went to college under the G.I. Bill, my Father helped me buy a bright, red Ford while I was attending college. While eating at *Purdue's Student Union* one day, a young girl tapped me on the shoulder to say hello and asked if I remembered her from Springfield. Even though I didn't, I reassured her that I did. She said she was attending the *College of St. Francis.*

CHAPTER 9
COURTSHIP

I faintly remember when I first met Midge. I had been double dating with Bob Delaney, who was dating Midge's older sister, Jean, whom by the way, he eventually married.

I did notice Midge as a cute, little high school candy girl at the *Lincoln Theater* in Springfield, Illinois. I was working at *Arch Wilson Clothing Store* only half a block from the theater. Having been the candy fanatic all my life, I use to venture to the theater for a chocolate bar. Looking back at life however, I think I went to the Lincoln to also gaze at Midge Dunham. Our conversations were very limited since she was still in high school and I was over twenty-one, just having returned from the war and overseas duty.

I only had glimpses of Midge while attending *Springfield Junior College* while I continued working part time at *Arch Wilson's* and buying my Hershey Bars at the theater.

After graduating from SCI, I attended *Purdue University*, and one day while eating in the *Union Building* Cafeteria, a young lady tapped me on the shoulder informing me that she was from Springfield. Although I did not admit remembering her or her name, I acted as if I did. Midge told me that she was attending the *College of St. Francis* and I promised to call.

Several days later, I went to the college to call on Midge. A nun answered the bell and I asked if I could see one of their freshman students from Springfield, Illinois, who's name unfortunately slipped my mind. The sister was not overly impressed by my presence and it took quite some persuasion for her to reveal Midge's name. I finally was allowed to speak to Midge for a brief moment, only to inform her that I would call on her for a date. I don't believe my wanting to date Midge impressed her very much and it was quite a while before I asked her out.

I attended *Purdue University* on my G.I. Bill, which paid for my schooling, and also issued me a monthly check for a little over $60. Periodically, my Dad would send me some additional funds. I will never forget our first date at a very elegant restaurant in Lafayette, Indiana. I wanted to impress Midge, although I knew the meal was extremely expensive for my limited budget. Looking back at that date, I realize that we would never have allowed our seventeen year old daughter to date a twenty-two year old army veteran. Although Midge never said anything, I now feel she must have been very uncomfortable. I know I was somewhat. Little did I envision us ever becoming husband and wife. At first our dates were somewhat sporadic, but as time went on and we started dating more frequently, I knew I was in love with Midge.

Midge and I at a dinner dance
at Purdue University in 1949.
The band was Duke Ellington.

After one year at the *College of St. Francis,* Midge transferred to the *Chicago Art Institute.* Midge attended school in Chicago, and I in Lafayette. It played havoc on our courtship. I missed Midge terribly, although I don't think the feeling was quite mutual. My enthusiasm for school was miserable, while Midge seemed to enjoy every minute of her schooling. In my senior year upon my return to Springfield for summer vacation, I went to work for the *State Highway Department* on Ash Street, while also working at *Walt Lynch's Clothing Store.* I continued working, not returning to school.

By this time we did consider getting married, although we did not tell anyone. One day I decided to move out of my parents' house and rent a small room from Aunt Lizzy, Midge's aunt. This, I know, hurt my parents immensely and we did not communicate for many months thereafter.

At Christmas of 1951, we informed my parents that we were going to marry and I still hoped to return to school. Our strained relationship continued, and although I loved my parents dearly, we never returned to the affection we shared prior to my moving away from our home. Having our own children now, I realize the tremendous hurt I imposed on my parents, and I regret forever having moved out.

We were married on June 14, 1952. It was a beautiful day weather wise. Many things went wrong, but to my satisfaction, I had very little to do with the arrangements. However, my parents totally excluded themselves from helping us.

Midge and I on our wedding day, June 14, 1952.

My Father never forgave me for leaving home and he threatened not to come to my wedding. To my great surprise, my Father, my Mother, my expectant sister, Edith, and her husband, Ken, did attend. We had a wonderful wedding breakfast at the restaurant now known as the *Chesapeake Seafood House*. The reception was held at the Dunham house at 208 W. Miller Street. The basement was decorated and most of the men gathered in the basement to play cards and consume various beverages, since that was the coolest place in this non air-conditioned house.

Our reception at the Dunham house.
From left to right, Ritter, Nellie (Midge's parents),
Me, Midge, my Mother and Father.

Since I was not a conversationalist, I spent most of my time in the kitchen with the Hall girls, Catherine and Mary Ellen. While I believe Midge circulated among the guests with her "Dunham charm", it was a dismal affair and I was really eager to leave on our honeymoon! The Hall girls prepared sandwiches and other food to take on our honeymoon, since they realized our funding was limited.

Midge and I traveled west to Arizona, Colorado, Oklahoma, and Texas, and returned back home with less than a dollar to our name. Upon our return, we purchased a two bedroom house from Midge's Uncle Tom. Within the first ten months, we became the proud parents of a 6 pound, 13 once baby girl named Joan.

CHAPTER 10
LIFE'S FULLFILLMENT

Year 2010:

At the age of 84 in the year 2010, I can count my many blessings. Even though I have faced some medical problems brought on by "old age" and losing my right leg a few years ago, I thank God for my many blessings and have tried to maintain an optimistic outlook on life. I have lived through many adversities and uncertainties and have been blessed throughout my life with Midge as my wife. We have been blessed with thirteen children and have been blessed with thirty grandchildren.

After being employed for four years for the State of Illinois, *Department of Transportation*, at the beginning of our marriage, I continued working in the field of Engineering in Dixon, Illinois and after two years, *Crawford, Murphy, and Tilly* in Springfield for twenty-two years. I helped design and construct sewage treatment plants, highways, and oversaw the building of *Camp*

Bunn, a Boy Scout Camp. At this engineering firm, I met and remained friends with my co-workers and colleagues throughout my adult life.

As our children grew, I was Cub Scout leader and volunteered many hours for *Blessed Sacrament Grade School, Griffin High School,* working bingo and the band program, and for *Ursuline Academy High School.*

In 1977, our twelve children presented Midge and I with a trip to Vienna, Austria for our 25th wedding anniversary. That same year, my Mother passed away. In October, 1977, my wife and I flew to Europe. Landing in Munich, Germany, we drove to Vienna, the place of my birth. This was the first time I had been back to Vienna since my 1939 departure. I felt as if I had only left a few days earlier.

We visited my cousin, Gusti, and the apartment my parents, sister, and I left nearly forty years ago. The apartment had not changed, but only aged. The grocery store where my Mother shopped was still located on the ground floor. I visited it with my wife and to question the present owner. As I introduced us to the man behind the counter, he ran to the back room yelling, *"Die Langfelders sind hier!"* An elderly gentleman came out to tell us that he was the same grocer who served my family over forty years earlier! Both of us were so emotional, that we cried and drank a glass of wine in celebration.

In 1978, after working for *Crawford, Murphy, and Tilly* for more than twenty years, I decided to run for political office. I had been a precinct committeeman and had been interested in politics, so I became a candidate for *Commissioner of Streets and Public Improvements.*

In 1979, after a close election, I was elected *Commissioner of Streets.* My Mother had passed away in 1977 and I knew how proud she would have been of me. I remember my pride when my Father was able to attend my inauguration. My Father would come to my office often and visit with me until his death in 1982.

While Commissioner, I implemented the first snow emergency route, curbside recycling with the "ugly" blue bins, banned leaf burning, and initiated the Madison Street corridor, which runs east and west in our fair city. I also served on several boards, like the *Springfield College (Benedictine) Board* and the *Salvation Army Board.*

In 1987, I ran for and was elected Mayor of Springfield. During my eight years as Mayor, the most important accomplishments were the change of the form of government, from the "Commissioner form" to the "Aldermanic form". Other accomplishments as Mayor were the development of the "Municipal Complex" and the redevelopment of the *Fiat Allis* property. During my tenure, a homeless shelter, *Helping Hands,* was started, two new fire stations were built, land acquisitions for a second lake were purchased, and a sister city alliance was conceived with Ashikaga, Japan.

In 1990, the *Springfield Municipal Band* was invited to the *Vienna Music Festival*. As Mayor it was my honor to accompany them as interpreter and emcee for the Band.

In 1995, I lost a third bid as Mayor, but continued to work, finding employment with the State of Illinois, where I had worked when Midge and I were first married. Ironically, I began working for the State as a family man and then retired from the State, from "Local Roads" at the *Department of Transportation* at the "young age" of 82! I always wanted to work longer than my Father who had retired at the "young age" of 78! I have always enjoyed working and was always pushing back my retirement age!

Looking back on my life, I have tried to show my children and grandchildren pride for their city. I have always tried to instill in my family hard work, honesty, and respect for oneself and community. While reminiscing, I have always felt my greatest accomplishment is my family.

Education was always our primary goal. Midge and our daughters, Joanie, Jamie, and Janice, are teachers in the Parochial School System, while another daughter, Jeannie, teaches in the Public School System. Our daughter, Judy, is a Professor of Nursing, and Jackie is a Speech Pathologist for the public schools. Our youngest daughter, Julia, is Marketing Director at a local bank. Our oldest son, John, is an attorney, while our son, Joey, recently retired as a Captain of the *Springfield Fire Department*.

Our son, Jay Paul, is in the insurance business and sons, Jimmy, and Josh, are elected public officials in Springfield. Our youngest son, Jacob, is in the entertainment business in New York City.

Our greatest blessing and reward is their success and contributions to society. Midge and I never measured success by financial reward, but rather by our children's achievements. In this regard, we have certainly reached our goal.

OSSIE LANGFELDER as MAYOR of SPRINGFIELD, ILLINOIS
1987 – 1995

EPILOGUE

Whether we are young or middle age,
each year is just another page.
But as we approach our senior years,
we reach for just a few more cheers.

Our frequent wish that tomorrow were here,
not realizing that we are ever so near.
The time, our clock is winding down,
and our body reminds us not to clown.

And as we sit and reminisce
about our heartaches and our bliss,
we pray and hope that what we have done
were things which brought happiness and fun.

We think and dream of our distant past,
and shed some tears 'cause it couldn't last.
We realize life was a wish for success,
and we would not dream of anything less.

And as I look back on my eighty-four year span,

although I can't recall how it began,

I dream of my childhood and the days of my past,

although they seemed to disappear ever so fast.

About the good times and the trouble I've seen

of what could have happened and what could have been,

I know that I've been very blessed

'cause I have a family, which is the best.

With Midge, who shared my woes and my joys

who presented me with seven wonderful girls and six wonderful boys.

If I again were young and dreamed of about my life,

I would have dreamed of no other than Midge for my wife.

With the thirteen J's, who are full of love,

I know they are truly a gift from above.

As I describe eighty-four years with one simple line,

My life has been great and ever so fine!

Ossie Langfelder

OUR FAMILY TREE

Oswald (Ossie) Langfelder

1926 –

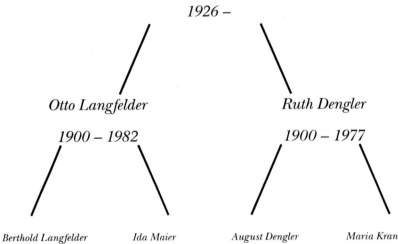

Otto Langfelder

1900 – 1982

Ruth Dengler

1900 – 1977

Berthold Langfelder
Hungary/Austria

Ida Maier
Czechoslovakia/Austria

August Dengler
1875 – 1921

Maria Kranzl
1881 – 1938

124

OUR FAMILY TREE

Mary (Midge) Dunham

1931 –

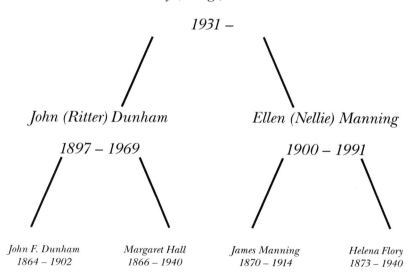

John (Ritter) Dunham

1897 – 1969

Ellen (Nellie) Manning

1900 – 1991

John F. Dunham
1864 – 1902

Margaret Hall
1866 – 1940

James Manning
1870 – 1914

Helena Flory
1873 – 1940

Breinigsville, PA USA
13 April 2011
259796BV00003B/1/P

9 781453 808726